THIS BOOK IS FOR

....

BORN

....

LOTS OF LOVE
FOREVER & ALWAYS

....

Made in the USA
Middletown, DE
05 October 2023

40298600R00084